Lil' Wiz

Rev. Dr. Terri Strong

Copyright © 2023 Terri L. Strong.

Page Layout and Biblical Paraphrase by Mary Catherine Nelson

All rights reserved. No part of this book may be reproduced, stored, or transmitted by any means—whether auditory, graphic, mechanical, or electronic—without written permission of both publisher and author, except in the case of brief excerpts used in critical articles and reviews. Unauthorized reproduction of any part of this work is illegal and is punishable by law.

ISBN: 979-8-88640-785-3 (sc)
ISBN: 979-8-88640-786-0 (hc)
ISBN: 979-8-88640-787-7 (e)

Because of the dynamic nature of the Internet, any web addresses or links contained in this book may have changed since publication and may no longer be valid. The views expressed in this work are solely those of the author and do not necessarily reflect the views of the publisher, and the publisher hereby disclaims any responsibility for them.

One Galleria Blvd., Suite 1900, Metairie, LA 70001
1-888-421-2397

Introduction

These quotes were written to remind my sons of all the things I tried to instill in their hearts while growing up. In training them in the way they should live, I wanted them to know that wisdom is more important than material things.

With outside forces being so strong, it is critical to strengthen our children inside. The title of the book says it all because the content is a little that shares a lot. It is also simple enough for all to understand and broad enough to cover a lot of life's lessons for ages from birth to over 100.

Hopefully, my sons have absorbed the wisdom that I have shared with them in the same way I sponged what my parents shared with me. I trust that everyone reading this book will relate to some of the material presented, enjoy the wit and wisdom, and find something useful for living their own lives.

For best results, a recommended dosage of the thoughts and wisdom herein is to read one of the fifty-two Lil' Wiz quotes with your children and your family for an entire week, along with the scripture references. Then reflect and discuss the meaning as a group. In this manner, each will have time to soak in and be fully absorbed. You and your family may very well develop related thoughts of your own.

Terri L. Strong

WEEK 1

God made all His creations to worship Him and Him only!

You must not worship any other gods except me."
Exodus 20:3

Let everything that breathes praise the Lord.
Psalms 150:6

WORDS...

WEEK 2

...are powerful. They have the power to create, build up, heal, tear down, and destroy. Therefore, be careful how you use them and listen carefully to other people's usage. Speak ill of no one, and live life so that no one can speak ill of you and be telling the truth at the same time!

One who is steadfast in righteousness attains life,
But one who pursues evil attains his own death.
Proverbs 11:19

The wicked talk of killing people.
But the words of good people will save them.
Proverbs 12:6

WEEK 3

NEVER LOSE SIGHT OF YOUR DREAMS. THEY ARE YOUR FUTURE'S REALITY

God began to do a good work in you.
And I am sure that he will keep on doing it until he
has finished it. He will keep on until the day Jesus Christ comes again
Philippians 1:6

WEEK 4

WHEN YOU SUCCEED TO MAKE EXCUSES, YOU FAIL. WHEN YOU FAIL TO MAKE EXCUSES YOU SUCCEED!

Always remember what is written in the
Book of the Teachings. Study it day and night.
Then you will be sure to obey everything that is written there.
If you do this, you will be wise and successful in everything.
Joshua 1:8

WEEK 5

IGNORANCE IS THE ESSENCE OF BONDAGE.

My people will be destroyed
because they have no knowledge.
You priests have refused to learn.
So I will refuse to let you be priests to me.
You have forgotten the teachings of your God.
So I will reject your children.
Hosea 4:6

WEEK 6

THE WORD OF GOD IS THE ESSENCE OF FREEDOM!

[32] Then you will know the truth. And the truth will make you free."

[33] They answered, "We are Abraham's children. And we have never been slaves. So why do you say that we will be free?"

[34] Jesus answered, "I tell you the truth. Everyone who lives in sin is a slave to sin.

[35] A slave does not stay with a family forever, but a son belongs to the family forever. 36 So if the Son makes you free, then you will be truly free.

John 8:32-36

WEEK 7

WHENEVER YOU HAVE A QUESTION, THERE IS ALWAYS SOMEONE WHO HAS THE ANSWER TO IT. DO NOT STOP SEARCHING UNTIL YOU FIND THE ANSWER!

My child, believe what I say. And remember what I command you. Listen to wisdom. Try with all your heart to gain understanding. Cry out for wisdom. Beg for understanding. Search for it as you would for silver. Hunt for it like hidden treasure. Then you will understand what it means to respect the Lord.
Proverbs 2:1-5

WEEK 8

IF THE TRUTH HURTS, LET IT. THE LIE YOU TELL WILL DO MORE HARM!

But those who are cowards, who refuse to believe, who do evil things, who kill, who are sexually immoral, who do evil magic, who worship idols, and who tell lies— all these will have a place in the lake of burning sulfur.

Revelation 21:8

WEEK 9

The mouth is a very useful instrument. One use is to admit when you've done wrong!

As the Scripture says,
"Anyone who trusts in him will never be disappointed.
Romans 10:11

WEEK 10

If a person makes a fool out of you the first time, they shouldn't have. If the same person makes a fool out of you the second time, they <u>should</u> have! The scripture says to "pray for those who spitefully use you," rather than let them keep using you.

You are happy when people hate you and are cruel to you. You are happy when they say that you are evil because you belong to the Son of Man.
Luke 6:22

WEEK 11

If you have an appointment at, say, 8:00 a.m., you must prepare and leave earlier than eight in order to arrive on time. Your goals in life should have appointment times and you should prepare early enough to arrive at them on time.

Don't be late for life! Set your "inner" clock so you will be on time. If for some reason you don't hear it, and wake up late, there is still time to catch up if you get started right away! Don't be late for life!

Procrastination is the thief of time!

You sleep a little; you take a nap. You fold your hands and rest. So, you will be as poor as if you had been robbed. You will have as little as if you had been held up.
Proverbs 6:10-11

You sleep a little; you take a nap. You fold your hands and rest. Soon you will be poor, as if you had been robbed. You will have as little as if you had been held up.
Proverbs 24:33-34

WEEK 12

There are more magic words than "please" and "thank you." Try "I can." They make things happen after they build your confidence.

Let the weak say, "I am strong."
Joel 3:10b

WEEK 13

NO ONE CAN SEE YOU WITH THEIR EYES. THEY MUST EXPERIENCE YOU WITH THEIR SPIRIT, EMOTIONS, AND FEELINGS. LET EVERYONE WHO ENCOUNTERS YOU HAVE A PLEASANT EXPERIENCE!

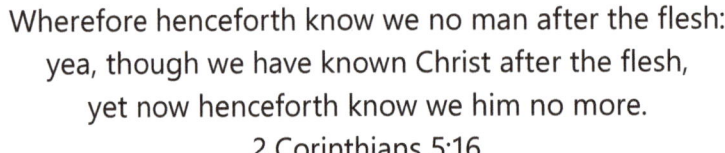

Wherefore henceforth know we no man after the flesh: yea, though we have known Christ after the flesh, yet now henceforth know we him no more.
2 Corinthians 5:16

WEEK 14

> **THE MOMENT YOU FEEL THAT YOU KNOW EVERYTHING, IS THE SAME MOMENT YOU BECOME A FOOL!**

Don't depend on your own wisdom.
Respect the Lord and refuse to do wrong.
Proverbs 3:7

WEEK 15

THE MOMENT YOU ADMIT YOU HAVE BEEN A FOOL IS THE MOMENT YOU BECOME WISE!

Do not fool yourselves. If anyone among you thinks he is wise in this world, he should become a fool. Then he can become truly wise,
I Corinthians 3:18

WEEK 16

> Do not treasure the things that are outside of you, but rather the things that are inside of you. This is the true substance of life.

Happy is the person who finds wisdom.
And happy is the person who gets understanding.
Wisdom is worth more than silver. It brings more profit than gold.
Wisdom is more precious than rubies. Nothing you want is equal
to it. With her right-hand wisdom offers you a long life.
With her left hand she gives you riches and honor.
Proverbs 3:13-16

It is better to get wisdom than gold.
It is better to choose understanding than silver!
Proverbs 16:16

WEEK 17

> God is not hard to find when you realize He's not lost; it's you!

But Christ died for us while we were still sinners.
In this way God shows his great love for us.
Romans 5:8

WEEK 18

JOHN 3:16
WHOSOEVER!

For God loved the world so much that he gave his only Son. God gave his Son so that whoever believes in him may not be lost, but have eternal life.
John 3:16

WEEK 19

Rain comes to make all things grow. It makes plants and trees grow on the outside and people grow on the inside.

And we also have joy with our troubles because we know that these troubles produce patience. And patience produces character, and character produces hope. And this hope will never disappoint us because God has poured out his love to fill our hearts. God gave us his love through the Holy Spirit, whom God has given to us.
Romans 5:3-5

WEEK 20

> You have all the patience you need. Let your prayer be to use it wisely!

Brothers, be patient until the Lord comes again. A farmer is patient. He waits for his valuable crop to grow from the earth. He waits patiently for it to receive the first rain and the last rain. [8]You, too, must be patient. Do not give up hope. The Lord is coming soon.
James 5:7-8

WEEK 21

Love knows no boundaries and has never been acquainted with hate.

Even much water cannot put out the flame of love. Floods cannot drown love. If a man offered everything in his house for love, people would totally reject it.
Song of Solomon 8:7

WEEK 22

The hierarchy of love is:

Love God

Love Self

Love Others

Jesus answered, "'Love the Lord your God with all your heart, soul and mind.'[d] 38This is the first and most important command. 39And the second command is like the first: 'Love your neighbor as you love yourself.
Matthew 22:37-39, Mark 12:29-31

WEEK 23

MAMA ALWAYS SAID,

"I DON'T CARE WHO DOES WRONG, YOU DO WHAT IS RIGHT!"

Stay away from the evil desires of youth.
Try hard to live right and to have faith, love, and peace.
Work for these things together with those who
have pure hearts and who trust in the Lord
II Timothy 2:22, I Timothy 5:10-11

WEEK 24

If you do something and it turns out wrong the first time, having done your best, you should not feel that time was wasted. But, if you did not give it your all, you should feel it was wasted. Try doing things right the first time and don't waste time!

If a person waits for perfect weather, he will never plant his seeds. And if he is afraid that every cloud will bring rain, he will never harvest his crops.

You don't know where the wind will blow. And you don't know how a baby grows in its mother's body. In the same way, God certainly made all things. But you can't understand what he is doing. Begin planting early in the morning, and don't stop working until evening. This is because you don't know which things you do will succeed. It is even possible that everything you do will succeed.

Ecclesiastes 11:4-6

WEEK 25

When you see the "milk" fall, start to "cry". When you see it "hit the floor," "stop and mop"

He prayed, "Abba, Father! You can do all things.
Let me not have this cup of suffering.
But do what you want, not what I want."
Mark 14:36

WEEK 26

Never let anyone influence you to do wrong with them. If you're going to do it, if you must do it, (PLEASE DON'T DO IT!), do it because it was your decision. When you make the decision to do wrong (PLEASE DON'T DO IT!), don't try to influence others to do it with you. Let it be their decision.

My child, sinners will try to lead you into sin.
But do not follow them.
Proverbs 1:10

WEEK 27

Put your hands at the sides of your eyes to block your peripheral vision. This is the way to focus on a goal. Otherwise, you might be distracted and delayed from reaching it.

I keep trying to reach the goal and get the prize.
That prize is mine because God called me
through Christ to the life above.
Philippians 3:14

WEEK 28

Life is simply the passing of time. Therefore, it is important to remember what you learned in elementary school:

"Use your time wisely." After all, it is your life!

I also realized something else here on earth that is senseless: The fast runner does not always win the race. The strong army does not always win the battle. The wise man does not always have food. The smart man does not always become wealthy. And the man with special skills does not always receive praise. Bad things happen to everyone.

Ecclesiastes 9:11

WEEK 29

All my life I've seen the sun shine after the rain, no matter how hard it stormed. Therefore, I learned to look for the brighter day after and not concentrate on the storms themselves. You can only be happy during the rainfall of life if you're confident and look forward to the brighter days that follow.

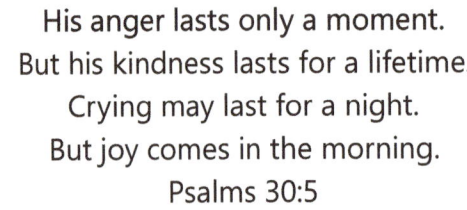

His anger lasts only a moment.
But his kindness lasts for a lifetime.
Crying may last for a night.
But joy comes in the morning.
Psalms 30:5

WEEK 30

When you blame others for a problem you will always look for <u>them</u> to solve it. However, if you find that they refuse to solve the problem, and you want it done, it's up to you to accept the blame, (even though it's not your fault) and take responsibility to solve it!

He could not find anyone to help the people.
He was surprised that there was no one to help.
So, the Lord used his own power to save the people.
His own goodness gave him strength.
Isaiah 59:6

Christ had no sin. But God made him become sin.
God did this for us so that in Christ we could
become right with God.
II Corinthians 5:21

WEEK 31

Say, two people are running in a political race and there are 100,001 voters of which <u>you are one of them</u>. And say, everyone has voted but <u>you</u> and the race is tied 50,000 to 50,000. That means you have the deciding vote. NEVER SAY your vote does not count! It could be the deciding one! VOTE!

We have freedom now because Christ made us free. So, stand strong. Do not change and go back into the slavery of the law.
Galatians 5:1

WEEK 32

Years ago, "they" locked slaves in chains and the slaves didn't like it. Yet most were passive and didn't run away. Today they lock criminals in chains and in "cages" so you know they don't like that! Still, they keep going back for more! Don't develop a slave or criminal mentality. They are one and the same.

You can follow sin, or obey God. Sin brings spiritual death.
But obeying God makes you right with him.
Thank God, you fully obeyed the things that were taught to you.
You were made free from sin, and now you are servants to goodness.
Romans 6:16-18

WEEK 33

Just when you think you "know it all", someone comes along and teaches you something you didn't know. Learning is a life-long process!

My child, hold on to wisdom and reason. Don't let them out of your sight!
Proverbs 3:21

Don't ever forget my words. Keep them deep within your heart.
Proverbs 4:21

Those who listen to me are happy. They stand watching at my door every day. They are at my open doorway, wanting to be with me.
Proverbs 8:34

WEEK 34

If ever you feel like a "square" in your "circle" of associates, get off that "block" and find the "hole' that you fit in!

You are not the same as those who do not believe.
So do not join yourselves to them.
Good and bad do not belong together.
Light and darkness cannot share together.
II Corinthians 6:14

WEEK 35

Chances are given and take. Sometimes you have to give them, and sometimes you have to take them. Sometimes others give you a chance and other times they might take a chance on you. Trust and be trustworthy.

Some friends may ruin you.
But a real friend will be more loyal than a brother.
Proverbs 18:24

WEEK 36

Discouragement is when others stand with you for a "cause" and in the "thick of it" you find yourself standing alone.

They have killed your prophets, and they have destroyed your altars. I am the only prophet left. And now they are trying to kill me, too.
Romans 11:3

WEEK 37

Bullets, Aids, and a lot of other deadly things have no one's name on them. However, someone just might want to label one of them with your name. Be Ve-r-r-r-r-ry careful about the company you keep!

A cruel man tricks his neighbor. He leads him to do wrong.
Proverbs 16:29

WEEK 38

I heard a man say that a body is used only to express life through. Express yourself: live!
Rod Parsley

A happy heart is like good medicine.
But a broken spirit drains your strength.
Proverbs 17:22

WEEK 39

> If you can't think of what to say, you probably need to keep quiet!

Even a foolish person seems to be wise if he keeps quiet. He appears to have understanding if he doesn't speak.

Proverbs 17:28

WEEK 40

If you have more to teach than you need to learn, then you need to talk more than you listen. If you have more to learn than you have to teach, then you need to listen more than you talk! Usually, most people have more to learn than to teach!

My dear brothers, always be willing to listen and slow to speak. Do not become angry easily.
James 1:19

WEEK 41

True class is when you can act like you're used to things, even when you're not! For God's sake, have some class!

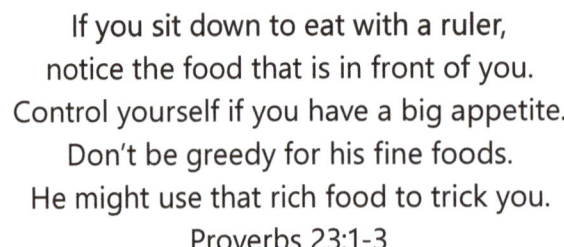

If you sit down to eat with a ruler,
notice the food that is in front of you.
Control yourself if you have a big appetite.
Don't be greedy for his fine foods.
He might use that rich food to trick you.
Proverbs 23:1-3

WEEK 42

Always test your friends.
Don't loan them money
and see if you remain friends.

Many people want to please a leader.
And everyone is friends with those who give gifts.
Proverbs 19:6

WEEK 43

IF YOU WATCH WHAT YOU SAY THEN

YOU WILL WATCH WHAT YOU DO!

DON'T USE PROFANITY!!!

A person who is careful about what he says keeps himself out of trouble.
Proverbs 21:23

WEEK 44

My father said when you are about to drive over a railroad track, always drive as far to the right as possible and never in the center. He said it's because that's the "road less traveled" and smoother. Take the road of life that is less traveled; the straight and narrow. In the long run it is smoother.

A good person stays away from evil.
A person who watches what he does protects his life.
Proverbs 16:17

WEEK 45

Churches, schools, and professions have one thing in common: there's trouble in every one. This doesn't stop you from working or going to school so don't let it stop you from going to church!

A storm will blow the evil person away.
But a good person will always be safe.
Proverbs 10:25

WEEK 46

Think quality not quantity. The best is not always the most expensive, but always be willing to pay for the best because it usually is expensive.

The buyer says, "This is bad. It's no good."
Then he goes away and brags about what he bought.
Proverbs 20:14

WEEK 47

From time to time, you will run across a person who, for no good reason, dislikes you. Don't take it personal!

If the world hates you,
remember that it hated me first.
John 15:18

WEEK 48

Most people or committees, if given one hour on a problem, spend 55 minutes talking about the problem, 5 minutes talking about the solution, and <u>no</u> minutes taking action! Don't be like most people. Be willing to spend 5 minutes talking about the solution and 55 minutes taking action! Because 9 times out of 10 you already know what the problem is and have some idea of how to solve it.

My brothers, if someone says he has faith, but does nothing, his faith is worth nothing. Can faith like that save him? ...So, you see that a person is made right with God by the things he does. He cannot be made right by faith only.

James 2:14, 24

WEEK 49

If ever you find yourself traveling way too fast through the streets of life, remember what I told my son when I was teaching him to drive:

"Brake Boy!!"

Enthusiasm without knowledge is not good.
If you act too quickly, you might make a mistake.
Proverbs 19:2

WEEK 50

REMEMBER WHO THE 10% BELONGS TO!

Honor the Lord by giving him part of your wealth.
Give him the first fruits from all your crops.
Proverbs 3:9

WEEK 51

IN ALL THAT YOU DO BE PRAYERFUL AND CAREFUL!

Stay awake and pray for strength against temptation.
Your spirit wants to do what is right. But your body is weak."
Matthew 26:41

WEEK 52

> Every part of life is like a seesaw ride; up and down, up and down, up and down. Have fun!

Everyone who wants to live the way God wants, in Christ Jesus, will be persecuted. People who are evil and cheat other people will go from bad to worse. They will fool others, but they will also be fooling themselves. But you should continue following the teachings that you learned. You know that these teachings are true. And you know you can trust those who taught you. You have known the Holy Scriptures since you were a child. The Scriptures are able to make you wise. And that wisdom leads to salvation through faith in Christ Jesus.

II Timothy 3:12-15

Your Lil' Wiz Notes

Your Lil' Wiz Notes

Your Lil' Wiz Notes

Your Lil' Wiz Notes

Your Lil' Wiz Notes

Your Lil' Wiz Notes

www.ingramcontent.com/pod-product-compliance
Lightning Source LLC
LaVergne TN
LVHW072128060526
838201LV00071B/4995